School

Helena Attlee

Commissioned photography by
Chris Fairclough

FRANKLIN WATTS
LONDON • SYDNEY

This edition 2008

Franklin Watts
338 Euston Road, London NW1 3BH

Franklin Watts Australia
Level 17/207 Kent Street, Sydney, NSW 2000

© 2004 Franklin Watts

ISBN: 978 0 7496 7925 5

A CIP catalogue record for this book is available from the British Library

Printed in Malaysia

Planning and production by Discovery Books Limited
Editor: Helena Attlee
Designer: Ian Winton
Consultant: Liz Burton, Head Teacher, St Ebbe's Church of England Primary School, Oxford.

The author, packager and publisher would like to thank the staff and pupils of St Ebbe's Church of England Primary School, Oxford for their participation in this book.

Franklin Watts is a division of Hachette Children's Books, an Hachette Livre UK company.

Contents

The school bus

Every day Elery waits at the bus stop with her Mum and her younger brother, Matthew. They are waiting for the school bus. The bus stop is just outside their house.

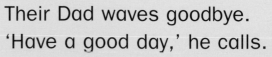

Their Dad waves goodbye. 'Have a good day,' he calls.

When the bus arrives, Elery and Matthew stand well back from the road until it has stopped moving. 'Good morning, you two,' says the bus driver as they climb aboard.

He waits for them to sit down safely before he sets off again. Elery sits at the front of the bus. She would like to talk to the driver, but she knows that she must not distract him while he is driving.

SAFETY FACTS

Sit down!

Always sit down on the school bus, and do not make too much noise. The driver needs to concentrate. If the driver is distracted there might be an accident.

Arriving at school

Soon they arrive at school. Elery sees her friend Fahema waiting to cross the road, and she stands up to wave. 'Sit down please, Elery,' says the driver. 'We're still moving.' When the bus is safely parked the children get off. 'Don't forget your bag, Matthew!' the driver reminds him.

Crossing the road

Elery watches as the crossing patrol lady helps Fahema to cross the road safely to get to school.

The girls know they are not allowed to go into the school by the main gate. The car park is busy at this time of the day, and it would be dangerous to walk through it. They use the side gate instead.

Car parks

Take special care in the school car park. If you have to cross the car park, remember that a car may back suddenly out of a parking space. Always stand back, as the driver may not have seen you.

Lots of the children cycle to school on their bikes. Marius and Ianto wear fluorescent jackets so that drivers will see them on the road. They lock their bikes carefully before they go into school.

When all the children have arrived, Mrs Godby, the school caretaker, locks the gate to stop strangers coming into the school.

Starting the day

Fahema and Elery hang up their coats and unpack their bags in the girls' cloakroom.

They go out into the corridor and run towards their classroom.
'Stop running, girls,' a teacher calls out.

SAFETY FACTS

Always walk between classrooms at school. If you run you might trip over and hurt yourself, or you might bump into other people and hurt them. Be especially careful not to run in the toilets or cloakrooms, where the floors may be wet and slippery.

Moving around the school

- Do not run.
- Do not push.
- Be especially careful near glass doors and windows.
- Do not make unnecessary noise.

Stand back!

The girls have to walk through the library to get to their classroom. When they reach the glass doors, they see a teacher walking towards them with a big pile of books. Elery opens the door to let her through, and Fahema stands back, too.

'Thank you, girls!' the teacher says.

A games lesson

The girls' first lesson today is games. The children go to the cloakrooms to get changed. In the girls' cloakroom Elery finds that she has forgotten her games kit. Luckily Mr Hughes, Elery's teacher, keeps a spare kit.

'You mustn't play games in your own clothes,' he tells her. 'You would get too hot, and your clothes wouldn't be very nice to wear for the rest of the day.'

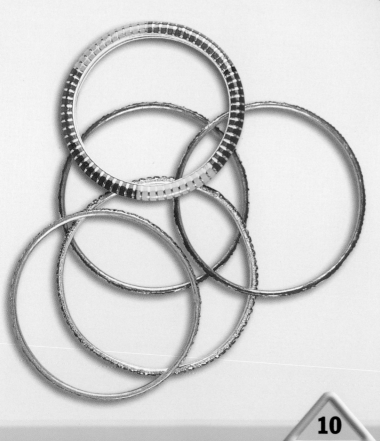

Fahema is wearing a ring and some bracelets. 'You'd better give those to me to look after,' says Mr Hughes. 'They might get caught on somebody else's clothes, and then you could get hurt.'

10

The girls are playing football today. Fahema is in goal. She goes to the cupboard to collect the goalie kit. When the ball hurtles towards her, she is very glad to be wearing shin pads and a thick goalie's shirt.

SAFETY FACTS

Always wear the correct protective clothing when you are playing sport. It is designed to stop you getting hurt.

In the gym

Matthew's class is having a PE lesson in the hall today. The children all go downstairs to get changed. They are careful not to push each other. They know that it could be very dangerous if someone tripped on a step and fell on top of the person in front of them.

The children help their teacher, Miss van der Zee, to put out the apparatus in the hall. When they have finished, she checks all the apparatus again to make sure that it is safe. Then she tells the children to put out the safety mats.

Sultan thinks that it would be a good idea to test the rope ladder himself by climbing up it.

'Get down, Sultan,' calls Miss van der Zee. 'I haven't checked that ladder yet. It might not be safe.'

Matthew realizes that he has some chewing gum in his mouth. He asks Mrs Walton, the classroom assistant, for permission to go and throw it in the bin. 'Good thinking, Matthew,' she says. 'You shouldn't be chewing gum at school anyway, and especially not during a PE lesson!'

SAFETY FACTS

Never eat sweets or chew gum during a games or PE lesson. You might swallow it and choke.

Breaktime

The bell rings for break, and Elery and Fahema go outside to play. Elery has brought her new compasses to school to use during maths. She wants to show them to Fahema. When Mrs Walton sees that Elery has brought the compasses into the playground, she is not pleased. She takes them away.

'Those are sharp and they could be dangerous, Elery,' she says. 'I will give them back at the end of break, but you mustn't bring them outside again.'

SAFETY FACTS

- **Never play with anything sharp as you might hurt yourself.**
- **Do not bring dangerous objects, like penknives, to school.**

Fahema watches the younger children play in the sand box. Helen starts to throw sand at her friend. 'Don't do that, Helen,' says Fahema gently. 'The sand might go into someone's eye.'

Fahema goes over to join some of the other children. They have all brought their skipping ropes to school. Elery watches their skipping game.

Suddenly, Fahema trips over the rope and scrapes her hand. Elery runs to get Mrs Walton.

SAFETY FACTS

If somebody hurts themselves at school, always tell a teacher or a classroom assistant straight away.

In the first-aid room

Mrs Walton takes Fahema to the first-aid room, and Elery goes along to keep her company.

'Oh dear, Fahema,' Mrs Walton says. 'We'll have to wash your hand and give you a nice, big plaster.'

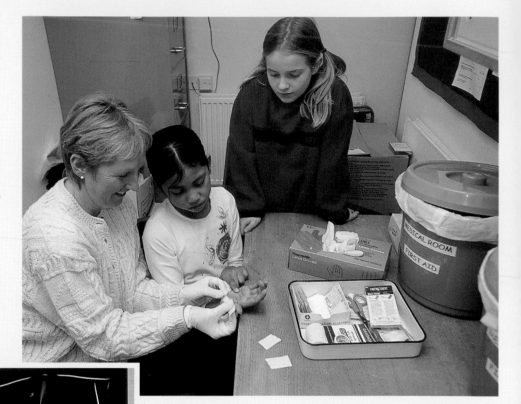

First aid box

First aid box

Mrs Walton unlocks a cupboard high on the wall of the first-aid room. 'This is where we keep the plasters,' she explains.

Pills and medicines

'There are lots of other things in there, too,' says Elery. 'Are they medicines?'
'Yes,' replies Mrs Walton. 'If anyone has to bring special medicine to school, we put it here until they need it.'

SAFETY FACTS

If you have to take pills or medicine to school, always give them to your teacher to look after.

'Why can't they look after it themselves?' asks Fahema.
'If we look after it, we can be sure that other children won't get hold of it,' says Mrs Walton. 'Sometimes children mistake pills for sweets, and that can be very dangerous indeed.'

Using tools safely

After break the children go back to their classrooms. Today Matthew's class is doing a history project. Matthew and Sultan are working together to make a model of a castle.

'Can we cut out the wooden pieces for our castle now?' Sultan asks Miss van der Zee.

'Yes,' she replies, 'but you will need to be careful. The saw is very sharp. Keep your hands well away from the blade.'

Scissors

Matthew needs some scissors to cut out a flag for the top of his castle.

'Here you are, Matthew,' says Miss van der Zee. 'Carry the scissors with their blades pointing downwards, in case you trip over.'

SAFETY FACTS

- **Always wear the right clothes for the job. If you are painting, wear an overall or apron to protect your clothes.**
- **Always take special care when using tools and blades. Work neatly and cut away from your body.**

A fire drill

Just before dinner it is time for a fire drill. Miss Forbes, the school secretary, presses the fire bell. It gives everybody a shock.

'Line up!' calls Mr Hughes, the teacher in charge of Elery's and Fahema's class.

The children line up quietly by the door.

Leave everything behind

Elery grabs her new pencil case, and Fahema picks up her reading book. 'No, leave things where they are! We haven't got time to worry about them,' Mr Hughes explains.

The children stand quietly in line. They know they must not talk during a fire drill. They stay in line and walk down to the playground. 'No talking,' Mr Hughes says, 'and no running!' When all the classes in the school have lined up outside, their teachers take the register to make sure that everybody is there.

Every school has several fire extinguishers. You must never touch them.

Dinnertime

Dinnertime at last! Matthew collects his lunchbox from the cloakroom. He is very hungry after his busy morning. He sits down next to Jack.

'Would you like one of my biscuits, Matthew?' Jack asks.

'Thanks very much, Jack,' says Matthew, 'but I have a nut allergy, so I have to be very careful about what I eat.'

SAFETY FACTS

Never swap the food in your lunchboxes. Some children have food allergies. Their parents choose their food with care. It could be very dangerous for them to eat something from your box.

The younger children eat their lunch at a separate table. Suddenly, one of them knocks over the jug of water that has been put there for them to share.

'Whoops!' says Mrs Palfreeman, the kitchen assistant. 'Let's mop that up before someone slips on it and hurts themselves.'

SAFETY FACTS

Always clear up spilt drinks or broken plates straight away.

Playground bullies

After dinner Sultan goes outside to play football with his friends.

'Hey, you don't need that,' says Tessa. She takes the ball and runs away with her friends.

Sultan doesn't know what to do. He wants the ball back, but he is frightened of Tessa and her gang. They kick the ball towards him, but when he tries to get it, someone pushes him over.

Bullying

Matthew has seen what is happening. 'That's bullying!' he shouts. 'Perhaps I should go and push Tessa for you.' 'No, don't do that,' says Sultan. 'There are lots of people in her gang, and you might get hurt.' They see Mrs Davies, another teacher, walking by. 'I know,' Matthew says, 'we'll tell Mrs Davies what happened.'

SAFETY FACTS

Tell a grown-up

Always tell a grown-up if you are being bullied. They will sort it out.

Mrs Davies gets Sultan's ball back. Then she takes Tessa and her gang to the head teacher's office. Nobody likes bullies, and Miss Burton, the head teacher, will be very angry with them.

Trouble with footballs

Matthew and Sultan start to play together. Sultan gives the ball a great big kick, and it sails up on to the roof of the classroom. 'What a pity,' says Matthew. 'We were just starting to have fun!'

'Don't worry,' Sultan replies. 'I can easily climb up there and get it.'
'No you can't,' says Mrs Godby, the school caretaker. 'It's higher than you think, and that drainpipe isn't very strong.'

Getting help

Mrs Godby goes off and fetches her ladder. She soon throws the ball back to the boys. 'Here you are, boys,' she says. 'Take more care of it next time.'

It's not long before Sultan kicks the ball right over the fence and on to the road.
'Oh no!' shouts Matthew. 'My Dad will be furious if I lose that ball.'

Matthew starts to climb over the school fence, but just then a teacher walks down the road. She picks up the ball and throws it back.
'You must never, ever climb over that fence!' she says. 'And be more careful with your ball. If a car had been coming, it might have caused an accident.'

Going home

It is nearly time to go home. Elery is not going on the bus this afternoon. Her auntie is collecting her. They are going to the shops to choose some new rollerblades for her.

Elery's mother has written a letter to Mr Hughes. She has told him that Elery will be picked up by her auntie today.

Mr Hughes

'My rollerskates are too small for me,' says Elery. 'Will you come with us to the shops, Fahema? You could help me to choose some rollerblades.'

'Sorry Fahema,' says Mr Hughes. 'I haven't had a note from your Mum to say that you are going home with someone else. I'm afraid you will have to go home at the usual time.'

'I suppose you're right,' says Fahema. 'Mum wouldn't know where I was, and then she would be really worried.'

SAFETY FACTS

Never go home with someone different, unless your parents have given you permission, and your teachers know all about it.

Glossary

Allergy If you have a food allergy your body is very sensitive to certain foods. If you ate them you would be very ill.

Apparatus The equipment for a particular job or activity, such as gymnastics.

Blade The flat, cutting part of a knife.

Bully Use strength or power to frighten or hurt a weaker person.

Choke When you choke, you cough and gasp because your breathing tubes are blocked and you can't breathe properly.

Compasses an instrument used for drawing circles.

Concentrate Give your full attention to something.

Crossing patrol Man or woman whose job is to stop the traffic so that children can cross the road to get to school safely.

Distract Take a person's attention away from something.

Fire drill Practising what you must do if there is a fire.

Fire extinguisher Special equipment for putting out fires.

First aid Simple treatment that you give someone who is hurt or sick.

Fluorescent Something that shines in the dark.

Medicine Pills or other substances given to people to treat or prevent illnesses and diseases.

Shin pads Hard pads used to protect the lower part of the leg during ball games.

Useful addresses and websites

The Advisory Centre for Education
www.ace-ed.co.uk
An independent advice centre for parents on behalf of their children. Its publications include a booklet called Tackling Bullying.

Child Accident Prevention Trust,
22–26 Farringdon Lane, London EC1R 3AJ
www.capt.org.uk
Provides downloadable factsheets on accidents to children.

Department of Health
www.dh.gov.uk
The Department of Health is active in the area of accident prevention and medicine safety.

Elmer the Safety Elephant
www.safety-council.org
An attractive Canadian website offering internationally relevant tips on traffic, school bus, internet, and railway safety for kids through games, activities and stories.

Kidscape
www.kidscape.org.uk
Kidscape is a registered charity that aims to keep children safe from harm or abuse. The site includes advice for young people and parents who are being bullied as well as publications and leaflets produced by the organization.

Royal Society for the Prevention of Accidents (RoSPA),
Edgbaston Park, 353 Bristol Road, Birmingham, B5 7ST
www.rospa.com
Provides information, training and resources, and has a special feature about playground safety.

Safety Centre
18 Carter's Lane, Kiln Farm, Milton Keynes, MK11 3ES
www.safetycentre.co.uk
Hazard alley at the Safety Centre is a purpose-built, interactive centre where children aged 7-12 can experience twelve hazardous scenarios in perfect safety.

Sustrans,
35 King Street, Bristol BS1 4DZ
www.sustrans.org.uk and
www.saferoutestoschools.org.uk
Sustrans co-ordinates the Safe Routes to School project, providing support for local authorities, schools and parents. It publishes newletters, teachers' packs, project guides and information sheets.

Young Transnet (YTN),
National Children's Bureau, 8 Wakely Street, London EC1V 7QE
www.youngtransnet.org.uk
An interactive, child-centred website which encourages children to carry out surveys about school travel and enables them to compare results with other schools.

The Child Accident Prevention Foundation
www.kidsafe.com.au
A nationwide Australian charity providing advice on the prevention of accidents in the home.

Child and Youth Health,
295 South Terrace, Adelaide, SA 5000, Australia
Tel +618 8303 1500. Fax +618 8303 1656.
www.cyh.com
Online resources and links for the latest news and advice about parenting and child safety issues.

Child Safety Foundation
www.childsafety.co.nz
A New Zealand website designed mainly for use by
parents, which promotes all aspects of pre-school and early primary school safety.

Note to parents and teachers
Every effort has been made by the Publishers to ensure that these websites are suitable for children, that they are of the highest educational value, and that they contain no inappropriate or offensive material. However, because of the nature of the internet, it is impossible to guarantee that the content of these sites will not be altered. We strongly advise that internet access is supervised by a responsible adult.

Index